Mansa Musa and Timbuktu: The History of the West African Emperor and Medieval Africa's Most Fabled City

By Charles River Editors

A 14th century atlas' depiction of Mansa Musa holding a gold coin

About Charles River Editors

Charles River Editors is a boutique digital publishing company, specializing in bringing history back to life with educational and engaging books on a wide range of topics. Keep up to date with our new and free offerings with this 5 second sign up on our weekly mailing list, and visit Our Kindle Author Page to see other recently published Kindle titles.

We make these books for you and always want to know our readers' opinions, so we encourage you to leave reviews and look forward to publishing new and exciting titles each week.

Introduction

A 19th century depiction of Timbuktu

Mansa Musa

"From the far reaches of the Mediterranean Sea to the Indus River, the faithful approached the city of Mecca. All had the same objective to worship together at the most sacred shrine of Islam, the Kaaba in Mecca. One such traveler was Mansa Musa, Sultan of Mali in Western Africa. Mansa Musa had prepared carefully for the long journey he and his attendants would take. He was determined to travel not only for his own religious fulfillment but also for recruiting teachers and leaders so that his realms could learn more of the Prophet's teachings." – Mahmud Kati, *Chronicle of the Seeker*

Recent research has revealed that the richest person of all time lived in the 14th century in West Africa and went by many names, including Kankan Musa Keita, Emir of Melle, Lord of the Mines of Wangara, Conqueror of Ghanata and the Lion of Mali II, but today he is usually referred to as Mansa Musa. Adjusting his wealth to modern values, he was worth about an estimated $400 billion as the Sultan of ancient Mali, which controlled the trade routes across the Sahara Desert.

About 6,000 years ago, the ancient Sahara was a tropical jungle with lush grasslands and substantial rivers until it moved north of the Equator as a result of tectonic plate movements. The seismic activity changed the location of land and the composition of the atmosphere. The African Humid Period seems to have ended relatively quickly, taking a couple of thousand years before being replaced by a much drier climate, and this started a process of desertification that forced many animals and human inhabitants to the outer edges of the immense desert. There would have been passages through the area that vanished as the harsh climate inexorably clawed at the mountains and hills, turning them into the sand that obliterated all traces of their ever having been there. By about 600 BCE, the terrain and habitat had become much less hospitable, so much so that it was no longer possible to use horses and oxen to carry commodities. As a result, trading became difficult and sporadic and slowly disappeared.

This all changed when camels were introduced to the Sahara, initially via Roman invaders and then with the Berber traders from Arabia moving across North Africa in search of gold and salt. As they reached the southern Sahel, they encountered the old established trading system and routes of the Garamantes, the people who handled the trade in and out of the Sahara from West Africa. The combination of the use of camels with the already re-established West African trade routes brought about rapid economic progress that resulted in the area supplying more than half the world's gold for more than 1,000 years, beginning around 400 CE.

Of course, this timing coincided with the rise of global trade routes such as the Silk Road and the beginning of Europe's Age of Discovery. By the 12th century, it was believed that far to the east, beyond the lands controlled by the Muslim armies, lived a powerful Christian king named Prester John in the land of India. While he was a king, he was also a priest ("Prester" means Priest and was supposedly the only title he took). His kingdom was believed to be grand and contained many wonders. Marco Polo looked for Prester John, and the Crusaders wanted to reach out to Prester John. Portugal's Henry the Navigator sent his ships out with explicit instructions of what they should do if they met Prester John, and on his historic voyages, Columbus carried two books, *The Travels of Marco Polo* and *The Travels of Sir John Mandeville*, both of which have long passages on Prester John.

The belief in the existence of fabled African kingdoms and kings ensured that real African kings were also shrouded in lore, and few would become as legendary as Mansa Musa. *Mansa Mansa Musa and Timbuktu: The History of the West African Emperor and Medieval Africa's Most Fabled City* looks at one of the most famous rulers of the Middle Ages and the development of the city. Along with pictures and a bibliography, you will learn about Mansa Musa and Timbuktu like never before.

Mansa Musa and Timbuktu: The History of the West African Emperor and Medieval Africa's Most Fabled City

About Charles River Editors

Introduction

    The Sahara's Predecessors

    Sundiata and the Voyager

    Mansa Musa as a Leader

    Trade in Mansa Musa's Mali

    The Greatest Hajj in History

    Timbuktu

    Online Resources

    Bibliography

Free Books by Charles River Editors

Discounted Books by Charles River Editors

The Sahara's Predecessors

"The Sahara was a spectacle as alive as the sea. The tints of the dunes changed according to the time of day and the angle of the light: golden as apricots from far off, when we drove close to them they turned to freshly made butter; behind us they grew pink; from sand to rock, the materials of which the desert was made varied as much as its tints." – Simone de Beauvoir, *Force of Circumstance*

Unsurprisingly, the Sahara, as dangerous as it is abstruse, is both the muse and setting of countless legends. These stories, which have been relayed from one generation to another for several millennia, mainly revolve around the lost oases and buried treasures of the Sahara, the most renowned of these defunct paradisiacal cities being the fabled Zerzura.

The Sahara's transition from savanna to desert is marked by 2 phases. The first took place between 4700-3500 BCE, and the second occurred between 2000 and 1600 BCE. Once the monsoons had headed back south and the winds returned to the Mediterranean, what remained of the diminishing grasslands, rife with bald spots and shallow lakes, swiftly vanished. By 2000 BCE, the Sahara was as dry as it is now. When the last of the lakes dried up about a thousand years later, many of the Saharan tribes, following in the footsteps of their ancestors, migrated north, south, east, and west, literally in search of greener pastures.

Steph Lulu's picture of a mountain carved by the wind

Those who moved up north are believed to be the progenitors of the Egyptians, Phoenicians, Greeks, Jews, Berbers, and Tuaregs, as well as Nubian (Cush), Ethiopian (Aksum), and Sudanese (Ta-Neti) tribes. The communities developed here spoke in languages and dialects similar to the Ancient Egyptian tongue. Those who journeyed south spawned the Dravidians of South India and the Bantus of South Africa, as well as ancestral Pakistani and Iranian tribes. Those who trekked eastward became the forefathers of the Yoruba, Mande, and the Dogon in West Africa. The rest, who went west, settled in what would soon become Babylonia.

One of the tribes that audaciously decided against seeking their fortunes elsewhere were the Garamantes, a plucky and exceptionally resourceful people who inhabited the 250,000 square miles of what is now the Fazzan province in southwestern Libya. Like the other lost tribes of the Green Sahara, virtually nothing was known about the Garamantes for a long time - historians had only the accounts of biased chroniclers, such as the 5th century CE Greek scribe Herodotus, as well as other Roman writers. Herodotus depicted them as uncultured, simple-minded farmers who coated salty grounds with humus (a dark, organic substance formed by a mixture of decomposed leaves and animal matter). An excerpt from Herotus' observations on the Garamantes explained, "[The Garamantes] avoid all intercourse with men, possess no weapons of war, and do not know how to defend themselves...[They] hunt the Ethiopian hole-men, or troglodytes, in 4-horse chariots, for these troglodytes are exceedingly swift of foot...They eat snakes and lizards, and other reptiles, and speak a language like no other, but squeak like bats..."

An ancient bust of Herodotus

The Romans are known to have fought with the Garamantes on several occasions, so not surprisingly, the descriptions they peddled of the Garamantes were far less flattering. Tacitus, a Roman historian from the 1st century CE, vilified them as "a wild tribe much given to plundering...nomads who wandered from one inaccessible encampment to another." Others portrayed them as depraved, subhuman brutes.

David Mattingly, a professor from Leicester, shines a brighter light upon the Romans' attitude towards the Garamantes: "Consider the epithets used to describe them: numerous, savage, fierce, indomitable...naked, miserable, tent- or hut-dwelling, scattered, promiscuous, lawless, receivers of booty...given to brigandage, black." Black slaves were derogatorily nicknamed "faex Garamantarum," or in English, "Garamantian muck." Mattingly adds, "The almost universally negative tone of these terms must be recognized for what it is – a mixture of preconception and prejudice."

Garama was the capital of the Garamantes, who first entered the limelight in the 4th century BCE. The vast city was only one portion of the gargantuan Garamantian Empire, which hosted numerous other towns, over 50 villages, and a smattering of other hamlets. An estimated 4,000 citizens resided in Garama during its heyday, and another 56,000 Garamantes were strewn throughout the 100-mile-long Wadi Ajal (the depression the empire was nestled in) and other "suburban satellite villages."

Besides the profits raked in from their exports, much of the Garamantes' wealth can be ascribed to their heavy involvement in the ghastly but lucrative business of the slave trade. In order to continuously replenish their stock of slaves, which could only be achieved through war or conquest, the Garamantes needed to be accomplished fighters. They preferred to attack with their cavalry, which consisted of thousands of horse-drawn chariots. The Garamantian warriors wore little armor, defending themselves with not much more than round wooden shields and javelins, but they were light-footed, sharp, and responsive. More importantly, the ambitious warriors were as fearless as they were hungry for power, galloping into nearby towns and villages to make off with valuables and hordes of hostages. The captives were then enslaved and hauled off to the coast, where they were auctioned off to the highest Roman bidders.

Considering the vigorous Garamantian economy, it is easier to understand how these people purchased both necessities and material items with ease, but how did they manage to sustain themselves in such an infernal and water-deficient environment? Obviously, far from being the savages they were made out to be by the Romans, they had to be innovative. During the time of the Garamantes, the Saharan surface was dotted with plenty of mineral deposits, primarily "white-crusted" calcium carbonate. These mineral deposits were leftovers of crystalline lakes that had been scorched dry by the beating sun. Most of the lakes had vaporized, but in certain sweet spots lay secret storage compartments of "fossil water" encased in underground "permeable" rock formations, also known as "aquifers." These aquifers would become their most precious resource.

The Saharan city of Carthage was another powerhouse that coexisted with Garama. Local lore claims that the ancient city was established by a Phoenician princess, Dido of Tyre, also known as "Queen Elissa." Dido was married to an affluent Phoenician named Sychaeus, who earned not only the admiration but envy of his peers, many of whom longed for his hidden cache of gold, which came in every imaginable form, from coins to columns of bullion bars and even solid hunks of pure gold. Even Dido's father, King Belus, and her brother, Pygmalion, regardless of their immense riches, pined after Sychaeaus's treasure.

To historians, the myth of Carthaginian Queen Dido is precisely that. They assert that Carthage was a Phoenician colony that truly began to hit its stride in 332 BCE, following the obliteration of Tyre at the hands of Alexander the Great. Surviving Phoenicians packed their sacks and headed to the Tunisian coast, and since the majority of them belonged to the aristocracy, they possessed the means to build a powerhouse quickly. The city became the beating heart of the Phoenician trade in no time. Earning the trust of the nearby Phoenician cities – Utica, Hippo Diarrhytus, Leptis Parva, and later, other North African cities, including Garama – allowed the Carthaginians to build a sound and fast-growing economy, brightening up the flourishing Saharan markets with locally-grown olive oil, fish paste, and other spices and seasonings. Still, it was their solid relationship with the merchants from the Iberian Peninsula – in particular, Canary Island and the British Isles – that they cherished above all, as they were their main suppliers of silver and tin. Tin, to the Carthaginians, was especially imperative, for the metal was needed to produce bronze.

The Carthaginians seemed to be born with a stellar sense of direction. Masterful Carthaginian sailors such as Hanno the Navigator braved the uncharted waters and secured for them a trade route to the Ivory and Gold Coasts of the continent, whereas Himilco the Navigator pushed his way north along the Atlantic, and with both a stroke of luck and skill, found his way to England. In an effort to stave off competitors, such as the Greeks, the Carthaginian seafarers concocted and circulated rumors about sea beasts and sirens who overturned their boats and ate their sailors in the Mediterranean Sea. There were even ludicrous stories about enchanted "killer seaweeds" floating around at the time. A navy was also built, not only to guard their maritime wealth, but to serve as their first line of defense.

Once the dust had settled, the Romans moved in to their new territory, swept up the ashes, and rebuilt the city on their terms. By the turn of the 1st century CE, Carthage, which was rechristened "Carthago" by its new conquerors, had become the second largest city in the western wing of the Roman empire. 200 years later, the Romans built 2 amphitheaters in the Tunisian city of El Djem. The first of the amphitheaters, originally shaped out of a type of limestone called "tufa," is the more inconspicuous of the pair, constructed sometime during the spring of the 3rd century CE. The sweat, blood, and tears poured into the construction of this unnamed amphitheater, seemed to have been fruitless, for it fell into disuse just decades later.

In 238 CE, the infamous "Year of the 6 Roman Emperors," Gordian I, one of the 6 emperors crowned in a span of 12 months, commissioned the construction of the second amphitheater roughly 4.5 miles north of its counterpart. The blueprints of the free-standing oval masterpiece, pieced together entirely by stone bricks that decided to forgo any foundations, were based upon that of the Roman Colosseum. The Tunisian amphitheater would not be much smaller than the Colosseum, the grandest amphitheater in all of Rome, with its larger axis measuring about 485.56 feet alone. Furthermore, the stone bleachers that would line the walls would stack up to a height of 118 feet, with its engineers aiming for a maximum capacity of 35,000 spectators.

Most would assume that the Roman Empire was at this point basking in the glory of its regained riches. In truth, the disastrous power dispute had left the Roman treasury on the verge of depletion. The struggling government could hardly keep itself afloat, left alone finance such a princely project. And so, with the project's managers unable to foot the mounting bills, the amphitheater was never finished. Be that as it may, this iconic amphitheater became the city's most recognizable landmark. Nowadays, the amphitheater, honored as a World Heritage Site in 1979, continues to be a well-visited tourist attraction, and it is so immaculately preserved that it was used as one of the backdrops in the 2000 Hollywood blockbuster *Gladiator*.

A picture of some of the amphitheater's ruins

Around the same time these amphitheaters were built, Saharan merchants introduced into their trade pack animals that would revolutionize Arabian mercantile industries. Referred to by locals as the "ships of the desert," domesticated camels, though associated with desert settings, are not native to the Sahara. Rather, they were transported to Africa from southeast Asia sometime between 3000-2500 BCE. By nature, camels are "individualistic," but docile creatures. Rarely did they travel in packs, which made them all the easier to capture. It was only through the domestication of these camels that they learned to live alongside one another.

Camels were initially used as a means of human and luggage transport, as well as self-producing vessels of milk. As handy as they were, their numbers paled in comparison to that of donkeys and horses. It was not until the solidification of the military and political standing of the

Saharan Arabians that they began to import camels into the desert en masse, and these camels were repurposed as desert war stallions. Trainers saddled their camels with heavy weights, mounted them, and steered them through obstacle courses that changed by the week. They also refined their diets to boost their speed on the battlefield.

The role of the Saharan camels was once again reoriented in the 5th century BCE. Now "draft animals," they entered the field of agriculture, transformed into 4-legged machines that dragged carts of seeds across the field, powered mills, lifted water from wells, and performed other grueling chores. It would take another 700 years for the trend of utilizing camels in trade to catch on.

Not only could camels bear up to a load of 661 pounds over long distances and close to 1,000 lbs over short stretches, making them the perfect mode of transport for miscellany of commodities, they were naturally built for the desert, rendering them superior to horses. Camels have webbed, lightweight feet that prevented them from sinking into the sand, allowing them to move more quickly. Additionally, camel feet are padded with thick soles; by each heel is a plump "ball of fat" that kept their feet cool against the prickly heat of the sand.

Camels continue to be prized for their ability to forgo food and water for up to 17 days. Through each exhalation, camels retain water vapor in their nostrils, which is then soaked up by the body as a self-preserving means to save water. Their humps, which contain their "concentrated body fat," trap the insulation heat resulting from fat in one place, allowing them to better withstand the heat. Lastly, the camel's 3 eyelids, bushy eyebrows, and thick, doll-like lashes all protect them from the glaring rays of the sun.

The Saharan merchants, allowing a great portion of their camel population to retire from the battlefield, fattened them up with wheat, dates, hay, and grass before assigning them to caravans. A caravan usually consisted of 1,000 camels or so, but some are known to have been as large as 12,000. Strapped with hulking parcels bursting with gold, salt, pepper, silk, cotton, and ivory, and occasionally tugging carts filled with shackled shipments of slaves, camels trekked across the Trans-Saharan trade routes, sand and gravel crunching under their webbed feet.

Holger Reineccius's picture of a salt caravan in 1985

By the 6th century CE, the prevalence of caravan trading in the Sahara had elevated a new tribe to prominence: the Tuareg. Like many civilizations of antiquity, the origins of the Tuareg are shrouded in mystery. Some believe them to be the direct descendants of the Garamantes, while a few consider them as a canny, creative, and spiritual people of Egyptian extraction. The consensus, however, is convinced that the Tuareg are traceable to the Berbers.

The Berbers themselves were rooted in a 10,000 year old ethnic group that Herodotus referred to as the "Caspians," an archaic tribespeople who made their homes by the southern and southwestern shores of the Caspian Sea. Among the Caspians was a faction of tribespeople who, disgruntled by the increasingly crowded state of their home, abandoned the motherland. They ventured out from what is now Azerbaijan and northwestern Iran and headed west, ultimately winding up on the edge of the Sahara. In time, the Berbers arose from the Saharan Caspians, cropping up in Egypt, Libya, Algeria, Morocco, the Canary Islands, Niger, and Mali.

The Berbers, along with the other Caspian tribes that emerged at this time, were not strictly of "Caspian" descent. Instead, they were a hodgepodge of tribes with members of Middle Eastern, European, and African stock, including in its roster Romans, Carthaginians, Turks, Arabs, Vandals, Byzantines, French, Italians, and Spaniards, all of whom had governed Berber territories at one point. As a consequence, the Berbers were not bound by any discernible political identity, nor were they ever defined by a "unified empire," for their lands were simultaneously ruled by its own governments. Even so, the Berbers shared a unique language called the "Tamazight," now considered one of the oldest languages still spoken, that belonged to the colorful Afroasiatic language family and came with a mélange of dialects. It is for this reason that the indistinguishable Berbers are no longer seen as a race, but solely as a language.

While the ancient Berbers continued to grow progressively divergent in terms of their local laws and customs, they upheld many of the same religious traditions, and passed onto their children the same folklore imparted to them by their ancestors. The belief system of the early Berbers was centered on a pantheon of gods, mostly pertaining to the spirits of Mother Nature. Later generations integrated elements from local African mythologies, as well as touches of Judaism, Hellenistic religions, and Iberian tenets.

It was only in the 9th century CE that the Berbers began to part from their millennia-old traditions and embrace the word of God. The term "Tuareg" was coined by the Crusaders, meaning "abandoned by God." Others attached to them the sobriquet "the blue men of the Sahara," as the characteristic indigo scarves they donned often tinged their skin with traces of blue. At the end of the day, it did not matter what those unfamiliar with their ways thought of them, for the honorable tribespeople were well-acquainted with their own identity. They called themselves the Imohag, or "free men."

A precise date of the Tuareg's emergence has yet to be pinpointed, but most historians believe that the Tuareg, then Berber caravan traders, first appeared in Fazzan, enticed by the unclaimed grazing grounds the area offered. It was only following what historians call the "Tuareg diaspora" that they began to spring up in other areas of the Sahara, such as Niger, Algeria, Mali, and Burkina Faso. They soon developed a Berber-inspired language they styled the "Tamachek," and even instituted their own Libyan-influenced script known as the "Tifinagh."

In the beginning, the "semi-nomadic" Tuareg lived separately in various clans around the Sahara. Each secluded village was made up of spartan, collapsible huts thrown together with weaved matting, timber frames, and spare fabrics. Each was ruled by its own tribal governing system until the wise and arrestingly beautiful Tin Hinan, her bronze skin as bright as the midday sun, arrived on a "milk-white camel" with her servant, Takamet, in the mountains of Algeria. It was she, the "matriarchal ancestress of the Tuareg," who consolidated them under one kingdom in the 4th century CE and crowned herself their first-ever queen.

Thanks to the Tuareg's nomadic background, particularly their mobility and their unmatched resilience in the heat, they leapt on the opportunity to become the "middlemen" of the Trans-Saharan trade. Once they had collected the consignments from their clients, they headed north for the Mediterranean coast. Upon their arrival, they handed off the goods to maritime merchants, who then proceeded to distribute the product internationally.

Another Saharan city that soon propelled itself into the vanguard of the fast-changing Trans-Saharan trade was Timbuktu. Located in Mali in the southern half of the Sahara, just 12 miles north of the Niger River, Timbuktu is, as Robert Launay, an anthropology professor at Northwestern University, puts it, a "port of entry through the desert to North Africa." Scott Neuman, a contributor to *National Public Radio*, explained, "For centuries, it was a trading crossroads between Europe and the Middle East, and later an outpost connecting the West

African coast with the continent's largely unexplored interior." Apart from its strategic location, many, taking into account the ample natural riches and picturesque landscape of Timbuktu, called it the "Jewel of the Sahara," and others refer to it as one of the "great ancient wonders of the world."

A 19th century depiction of Timbuktu

It was in the 1100s that Timbuktu became recognized as a permanent settlement. As the original trade routes became disrupted by foreign competitors, the Timbuktuese pounced on the chance to emerge as a "transport hubs" for passing caravans. 2 centuries later, the city was absorbed into the Mali Empire. No longer known simply for its trading prowess, it was now a coruscating "cultural mecca" populated by talented artists, craftsmen, scholars, and other brilliant minds. Its resplendent library, which contained a wealth of Islamic, African, Greek, Roman, and other one-of-a-kind manuscripts, as well as its spectacular trio of mosques, put the city on the map as one of the most prestigious learning centers on the continent. As the schools and universities in the city multiplied, young students and aspiring scholars from near and far poured into Timbuktu, with many receiving scholarships generously provided by these affordable institutions.

Medieval Timbuktu was also overflowing with other prized products, namely salt and gold. Europeans were especially tantalized by the twinkling troves of dhahab that lay hidden in the city. When Mansa Musa, as King of Mali, discovered these desirable deposits in 1324, he would milk the mines with such might and vigor that by the next decade, the price of gold took a dive that failed to mend itself for several years.

Sundiata and the Voyager

In medieval times, Ghana (called Wagadu) and Mali were much closer to modern Mauretania and were inhabited by many different factions of the Mandinka Tribe, a hunter community. The Mandinka leader was said to have been descended from Bilal ibn Rabah, who had been a companion of the Prophet and gave rise to the Keita dynasty. They were the people who discovered gold at Bure and Bambuk, and they were soon threatened by Sumanguru Kanté, the sorcerer King of the Susu who ruled Kaniaga and was making a ruthless effort to take control of all the trade routes.

Around 1230, a leader emerged in the form of a prince of one of the minor Mandinka-speaking tribes. Very little is known about him except that he was a physically challenged child who worked intensely to overcome his initial inadequacies. There are also remnants from the transcription of an oral history called *Sundiata: An Epic of Old Mali*.

"Fear enters the heart of him who does not know his destiny,

whereas Sundiata knew that he was striding towards a great destiny."

Sundiata Keita became a warrior and gathered followers from many of the tribes before defeating Sumanguru in the Battle of Krina at Koulikoro in 1235. The oral history claims that Sundiata discovered that Sumanguru's sacred animal was a rooster. Sundiata poisoned the tip of his arrow with a cock's spur, and when he wounded his foe, Sumanguru fled from the field and deserted his army. The victorious Sundiata marched his troops to Sumanguru's capital, Sosso, and burned down his castle, including his "magic tower."

After the victory, Sundiata gathered all the Mandinka tribes together for a great assembly to create the Gbara, a deliberative body. This was formed by Mali, Mema, Wagadou, and "a cooperative assembly of all allied territories, including the conquered tribes' which was styled 'the Twelve Doors of Mali.'" The population was all assured of having a place in the land distribution, and they all took an oath to support Sundiata, his descendants, and the Keita dynasty. Their territory was named Mali, or Manden Kurufaba, meaning "where the kings live" and it was formed by 28 clans uniting under a Kouroukan Fouga (division of the world) held in 1235. The Gbara consisted of 32 positions called "farbas," and they controlled the following portfolios: Defense, Islamic Affairs, Trade, Governance, and others. Senior appointments were made, including the official "griots." These very important storytellers were powerful historians who held the oral history of the tribes in their memories.

The first meeting agreed on certain governing principles:

- There was a prohibition on maltreatment of any enemies defeated in battle and any slaves.

- Women were encouraged to apply for government posts.
- Guides were formulated about mutual respect between clans as spoken about in the Oral Epic. The progressive nature of this discussion is shown by one of these guides being: "I give the Kouyatés the right to make jokes about all the tribes, and in particular about the royal tribe of Keita."
- A fixed exchange rate would be agreed for certain common products.

    Gold: 4.5 grams = 1 mithqal or dinar [£144 today]

    Salt: One camel load = 10 dinars in the North and 20-40 dinars in the South

    Copper: 60 bars = 100 dinars

At the age of 18, Sundiata Keita was chosen and crowned under the name Mari Djata (Prince Lion). The following 20 years of his reign brought stability, relative peace, and an enormous growth in territory, trade, and wealth. Islam was the religion of the wealthy ruling classes, but it was not imposed on anybody.

Sundiata chose Niani as his capital, which was well situated near forests and navigable rivers and enabled him to build Mali as the key trading capital of West Africa. He was supported by loyal tribal leaders and established Arab traders as he steadily expanded the area under his control, judiciously allowing a mix of local chiefs and carefully chosen appointed governors so that the whole Mali Empire functioned as a coalition of independent kingdoms. However, he died in 1255, either by drowning or due to an accident involving a poisoned arrow while he was hunting.

Sundiata was succeeded by his three sons. The first was Uli, a mediocre leader who reigned for 15 years. Uli was followed by Wati, whose rule of four years was disastrous. In 1274, Wati was replaced by Khalifa, who was not only a really poor, dissolute and pathologically mean ruler, but was suspected of being mad. After a popular revolt, Sundiata's half-brother, Abubakari I, took the throne sometime between 1275 and 1280, and though he did restore some semblance of order and balance to the Mali Empire, he was simply a puppet of the elite.

In 1285 Mansa Sakoura usurped the throne. He was originally a slave from the Keita clan, but after those people had been freed, he became a competent and brave ruler who won the hearts of the people. He added Takedda, a significant city that produced copper, to the empire, but he was was killed by a robber while returning from the hajj. He was buried with all due regal honors.

In the wake of Mansa Sakoura's death, the Gbara intervened, and in 1300 they chose Sundiata's nephew, Ko Mamadi, as Mansa. He was succeeded by his son, Mohammed Ibn Gao, in 1305, and thus began a golden era for Mali following a tumultuous period.

In 1310, Mansa Abubakari II came reluctantly to the throne. Known as "The Voyager," he also had his eyes set on growth and development, but not simply on land. According to accounts, Abubakari II dispatched an exploratory fleet of 200 ships to cross the Atlantic and find the "other side" of the great Senegal River. One lone ship returned, and the captain reported back, "Yes, Oh Sultan, we travelled for a long time until there appeared in the open sea a river with a powerful current…the other ships went on ahead, but when they reached that place, they did not return and no more was seen of them…As for me, I went about at once and did not enter the river."

This was simply too much for the ambitious ruler, who immediately ordered a larger fleet for the journey. This time, he would send 2,000 ships full of men and another 1,000 ships carrying water and provisions, and he would go with them. Thus, he installed his nephew, Musa, as the caretaker of the empire and headed off on the expedition. When a year passed and Abubakari II had not returned, Musa became the 10th Mansa of Mali. He would spend the next 27 years spearheading the most spectacular growth of his empire.

Mansa Musa as a Leader

When Mansa Musa took power, the Mali Empire stretched from the Atlantic Ocean to Lake Chad, comprising parts of modern Niger, Nigeria, Mali, Burkina Faso, Gambia, Senegal, Guinea-Bissau, Guinea and Mauritania. By the end of Mansa Musa's reign, it would include Timbuktu, Gao, and Ghana. The Sahara "Sahel" formed the northern border, and the tropical equatorial forests ran along the southern edge.

Mansa Musa proved to be an excellent administrator, and he reinforced the decentralized structure the Gbara had instituted.

- A local village, town or city elected a village master (dougou-tigui) according to the bloodline of the founder of the settlement.
- The county level was governed by a county master (kafo-tigui) appointed by the provincial governor.
- Governors of provinces or states (dyamani-tigui) were scrutinized by officials in the capital. The citizens elected them but the Mansa had to give his approval and conducted a certain amount of oversight.

If Mansa Musa had some kind of reservation about governance, he could appoint a "farba" to the area. Newly annexed territories or those conquered during war would initially be governed by a "farba" until Mansa Musa was happy with the level of acquiescence, after which the dyamani-tigui was confirmed or another one was elected. In the case of unrest, or if an area was designated as essential to one of the trade routes, the "farba" remained in control.

Being a "farba" was considered very prestigious, as the duties included delivering regular reports, collecting taxes, and ensuring that the local law did not conflict with laws promulgated from Niani. A "farba" could also remove a native administrator from his post and played an important role in mobilizing any troops needed.

A gathering of administrators was held annually at the Sultan's palace and Musa was an exceptionally gifted leader in his handling of disputes and complaints. He introduced the best principles of Islamic law into the justice system. He spoke and read several languages apart from Arabic and he was very farsighted in his decisions. An example of this was that he did not attempt to place the gold producing provinces under his direct control but contented himself with sending emissaries to collect his tributes. His rationale when he was questioned on this practice, was that land controlled by its inhabitants, remained more productive than land ruled under duress.

Musa inherited a full-time, professional army served by a quota of fighters who had to be free men, from each clan. In his time the army was 100,000 strong. This included a cavalry of 10,000 men. The army was divided into a section responsible for the Northern border, commanded by a Farin and a section that was based fairly close to the capital, which was responsible for the Southern border, under the command of a Sankar.

The infantrymen were "sofa," quiver men, divided into groups of 10-20 men (kèlè-kulu), commanded by a Kèlè-kulu-kun-tigui. 10 groups together, consisting of 100–200 men, were commanded by a Kèlè-bolo-kun-tigui, and they formed a "war arm" that reported to a kèlè-kun-tigui. He might be in control as an overall kun-tigui or tribe master, or he might in fact also have to report to a higher officer, a "war tribe" master. The state equipped the "sofas" with weapons, and they carried bows, quivers and poisoned arrows, shields, and stabbing spears called "tambas." One spear man was supported by three arrow men, while the cavalry were usually Mandinka nobles who formed a Seré consisting of 50 horsemen commanded by a Kèlè-kun-tigui. The cavalry carried swords, lances, and javelins as well.

Although the army did report to the emperor, they all answered to the Gbara. There is surprising little information available about the top-ranking generals, but they must have quite enormously competent and successful, and they were certainly entrusted with the empire's security. During Mansa Musa's reign, a General Sagaman-dir is mentioned several times as a major military player. 24 cities were annexed to Mali during Musa's reign, and an attempt to conquer Timbuktu from Musa while he was on his hajj was dealt with swiftly in his absence.

Mansa Musa was at the head of a smooth administrative and military machine, and he was definitely an imperialist with his interests based on serving the ruling classes. He encouraged and supported young students to travel to the centers of learning in Fez and followed their progress closely. He also supported the development of higher learning in major towns like Djenne and Timbuktu. As a devout Muslim, he introduced the observation of Eid nationally and mandated five prayer times daily. He was observant himself and always supported education about the Qur'an in the specially established madrasas in every village. In this way, the empire played a major role in the spread and growth of Islam thanks to Mali's position as the center of trade in

West and North Africa.

Trade in Mansa Musa's Mali

Mining is one of the most ancient industrial endeavors. Digging the earth for gold, copper, silver, and other ores was established in Egypt around 4000 BCE, and by 1000 BCE it had spread to West Africa. Initially, it was closely associated with the religious belief systems of the people doing the mining - in the traditional religion of the early Berber inhabitants of the Kingdom of Wagadu, the belief was that a black snake god, Bida, blessed the land with replenished gold so long as there was an annual festival during which a virgin would be sacrificed to the god. One year, the chosen virgin's lover, Maadi, killed the snake with his saber, and a dreadful drought followed and all the gold mysteriously moved to Bure, at the headwaters of the River Niger. The ancient kingdom fell.

A historian explained the importance of mining and its religious significance: "Because ores abound in nature, the process of ore procurement in Africa involved negotiations between the living, the dead and the deities through the mediation of intermediaries such as spirits of the land. For the living to cross the nature–culture boundary to extract ores from the earth's belly, a number of rituals and taboos were conducted to propitiate ancestors. There are few archaeological traces of rituals associated with mining. However, ethnographically, in most parts of sub-Saharan Africa from the Dogon of Mali in West Africa to the Njanja of Zimbabwe, miners used medicines to neutralize malevolent influences during the process of mining." (Chirikure 2013).

By the time the Arabs conquered West Africa, their monetary system was founded on gold, and the headwaters of the Niger and the Senegal were providing a lucrative supply. Most of the inhabitants were hunter-farmers, but they all made a healthy second income by panning for alluvial gold, and when gold deposits were also discovered at the Bure and Bambuk mines, the already lucrative trade received a shot in the arm. Mali literally supplied the West with most of its gold for nearly 800 years.

Of course, gold was in demand all over the world, and travelers through West Africa were delivering reports of its availability in the "Land of Gold" as they returned to Europe and the North Islamic states. James Anderson explained in *Daily Life Through Trade*, "For instance, geographer al-Bakri described the eleventh-century court at Kumbi Saleh, where he saw gold-embroidered caps, golden saddles, shields and swords mounted with gold, and dogs' collars adorned with gold and silver."

The Western world's demand for gold was based not only on jewelry and ornamentation, but also for coins being minted throughout Europe. As far as Africa was concerned, this was especially important when it came to Spain and Italy, and in the 15th century, Portugal's Prince Henry the Navigator would set his sights on exploring the Atlantic seaboard mostly due to rumors of gold-plated streets in places like Timbuktu.

Perhaps not surprisingly, Mansa Musa kept a tight hold on gold production. The miners were not encouraged to become Muslims because the production of gold required the use of traditional magical practices often involving medicinal potions that were anathema to Islam. The agriculturalists did "placer" mining usually after the rainy season, working the alluvial deposits in the river headwaters, stream beds or glacial deposits, usually producing gold dust. The lode or rock mining actually took place in the mines of Bure, Bambuk, and Akan, and the location of these mines were carefully protected by locals and not revealed to the actual traders. Men, women, and children were all involved in the process, as men would dig for ore in the mines or dive for the sand carrying alluvial gold, and the women and children would do the winnowing. The children might even work the shallow streams on their own. Chirikure explained:

> "Because mining involved crossing the boundary between the surface and the belly of the earth, it was seen as a dangerous activity, characterized by many unknowns. Miners across Africa and elsewhere often required the intervention of the deities via intermediaries such as spirit mediums. Medicines were an important part of the mining ritual, for good medicines kept malevolent influences at bay while making it easier to find ore. In the African ethnographic record, miners did not always manage to find good ores; there were instances of failure. Under such circumstances, offerings and sacrifices were made to the ancestors, e.g., in the form of beer or chicken. Once ancestors were propitiated, the earth would release the ore. Therefore, mining required the intervention of both the dead and the living to help cope with uncertainty. The involvement of ancestors was important for another reason; mining took place in nature, conceptually away from the realm of culture. In this liminal [sic] space, it was only the ancestors who could guide the living. Furthermore, amongst many societies, the land on which mines were located was also under the realm of ancestors, who made it rain, and made land fertile and productive. Gold mining seems to have differed from copper and iron as far as rituals and taboos were concerned. It relied heavily on the labour of women and children and yet involved substantial underground excavation . . . Why did different communities treat this metal differently? Presumably, this stemmed from the fact that gold exists in pure form in nature, thereby contrasting with copper and iron that underwent dangerous heat-mediated chemo-thermal transformations to produce usable metal."

All the gold belonged to the king and nuggets had to be surrendered to the empire. The agriculturalists would be given gold dust equivalent to the nuggets they deposited, and trade was only allowed in gold dust, which would be secured in large bags and loaded on camels.

The cost of the gold was one thing, but money made from taxing the trade was the greater source of income. Travel across the Sahara was not easy, nor was it particularly safe, so certain trade routes became established and popular, primarily dictated by the availability of water and secondly shelter. There was always a trustworthy, skilled guide who could navigate the wilderness of roadless, signless, shifting sand dunes. The support structures of fresh camels, and the markets to sell and buy goods, provisions, banking services, doctors, guides and security guards gave rise to trading towns like Timbuktu, Gao, Sijilmasa, Kumbi Selah, and Aoudaghost. Goods arriving at these centers would be taxed, goods leaving them would be taxed, and that was directly responsible for Mali's abundant wealth.

The English word "salary" derives from the word "salt," a byproduct of how important a commodity salt was in antiquity. Salt was often used as a payment for work or goods received, in part because salt was scarce and not generally available. It is important for health and is the main source of sodium and chloride ions for people, essential for nerves and muscle function. Salt helps transport body fluids, assists in maintaining a healthy blood pressure, and acts as a disinfectant that can be used for cleaning all kinds of wounds.

Perhaps most importantly for the ancients, salt was a preservative, particularly in hot climates. Preserved food could be conveyed over greater distances, food could be stored, and people soon discovered that it enhanced the taste of almost everything they ate.

West Africa had an abundance of gold but no salt, while North Africa had many sources of salt and no gold, so the exchange of these two vital commodities formed the basis of the extraordinarily successful and rich trading caravans that crossed the Sahara. Most historical writers say that gold and salt were equal commodities in term of value. Kurlansky, in his book about salt, noted that salt and gold had a roughly equivalent value for many centuries.

There were different sources of salt, and not all salt was equal. Sea salt was easiest to obtain, but it did not travel very well and could be spoiled before it reached its destination. Amersal salt, used in animal feed, was also loose and did not travel well. Salt derived from the ashes of burnt plants was reasonable, but this salt was not rich in sodium chloride.

The best salt was found in the beds of old lakes and in salt rock which had to be extracted from a salt mine. Idjil in ancient Ghana had an excellent mine, which fell to Mali in the 13th century, and in North Mali itself, the Taghaza salt mine was an exceptional source. By the mid-16th century, the attention shifted to Taoudenni's mines.

Mining salt was labor intensive and difficult, and it took a major toll on the miners due to skin exposure to the corrosive material. These workers were often slaves, and they were counted on to carve great chunks and then shape them into slabs weighing about 200 pounds each. These were loaded onto camels, with one slab on each side, and transported to trading centers. According to Ibn Battuta, the best known of the explorers and writers of the region, the camel trains would contain an improbable 1,000-12,000 camels at a time. It seems an impossible number to manage considering that these journeys could often take a month or even more, but either way, the caravans would have been impossible without the mysterious "ships of the desert," the camel, which could actually go for ten days without water. It is quite likely that these huge caravans would be made up of traders with smaller herds that would all travel together for the sake of safety and companionship on what was always a hazardous and dangerous journey. If the caravan encountered rain or heavy mist, the salt had to be protected and carefully dried out before being reloaded, to avoid the slabs crumbling. At one of the large trading points, the slabs would often be loaded onto boats or pirogues sailing on the Niger and Senegal Rivers to the Gulf of Guinea or along the many tributaries inland. Sometimes there would be a depot where each slab would be cut into many smaller portions and then carried by porters to smaller village destinations.

Gold and salt were the main commodities, but there were many other goods. Caravans traveling north carried gold, ivory, ostrich feathers, ambergris, kola nuts, hides, and slaves, while caravans heading south brought salt, textiles, copper, silver, ironware, spices, books, paper, wheat and fried fruit.

Silent trade is described as the way gold and salt were typically traded. The traders of the commodities often did not have a language in common, which made things difficult since there was a need to keep the source of the product as much a secret as possible. Herodotus, the ancient Greek historian, wrote about the traditional way of solving this problem in West Africa when he described how the seafaring Carthaginians traded with a nation "beyond the Pillars of Hercules." In essence, there were particular places away from the villages, such as a river bank or crossroads, that were demarcated as trading places. The first trader would arrive with his goods and display them on the ground, perhaps in several piles if there were several products available. He would then withdraw a fair distance and out of sight, where he would give some kind of signal, such as beating a drum, blowing a horn, or creating a fire to indicate that there were goods ready for inspection. The second trader would approach the spot, examine the offerings, and leave a certain amount of gold or salt in a pile next to the goods he was interested in before withdrawing. The first trader would then come and have a look at the offering, and if he was happy, he would depart with the proffered gold or salt. If he was not happy, he would simply withdraw, leaving the second trader to increase the offering. This would continue until both were happy and one would leave with the goods. Often the traders would then depart for the local market to buy other goods before returning home.

Given this description and the level of trust involved in such a transaction, as well as the lack of proof of the quality of the goods (such as the type of salt or the purity of the gold), modern historians still debate if traders conducted trade this way.

The Greatest Hajj in History

"An ancient Tamacheq saying from Mali still echoes amidst the sun-scorched mud houses and desert sands of Timbuktu: 'Salt comes from the north, gold from the south, and silver from the country of the white men, but the word of God and the treasures of wisdom are only to be found in Timbuktu.'" - Thabo Mbeki, speaking at a fundraising dinner in April 2005.

17 years into his reign, Mansa Musa decided to make his pilgrimage to Mecca, a goal for devout Muslims across the world and one of the five Pillars of Islam. Every Muslim who is able and has the means is to make the hajj, which involves a physical and spiritual journey to the Kaaba, the House of God, in the holy city of Mecca.

It took almost as long to plan this enormous undertaking – two years – as the journey itself, because Mansa Musa decided to do it in such a way as to place Mali on the map, literally. His years of careful administration had brought his empire to the point that further development required more contact, more trade, and more exposure to the rest of the world, particularly Europe, North Africa, and West Asia. Mansa Musa consulted one of his "shaykhs," or elders, for a propitious date for such an endeavor, and the elder replied, "You should wait for the Saturday which falls on the twelfth day of the month. Set forth on that day, and you shall not die before you return safe and sound to your residence, please God." If Mansa acted on the advice, then they would have departed in either February or August, as they were the only two months in 1324 with a Saturday falling on the 12th and there is documentary proof that they left in that year. Had they left in August, it is doubtful they would have arrived in Mecca in time, so they probably left in February.

Regardless of its timing, it was truly a spectacular hajj. Mansa Musa planned the logistics of this journey meticulously to ensure stability in his absence, including inviting senior officials from every province as well as leading and influential citizens, such as doctors, teachers and senior "griots," to accompany him. In turn, they made arrangements for their responsibilities and interests to be protected while they were away.

Mansa Musa placed his elder son, Maghan, in charge of the empire and also left his most favored military officer, General Sagaman-dir, at the head of the army in case his son needed any serious backup. His favorite wife, Inari Kunate, with her own retinue of 500 attendants, accompanied him. The emperor also let it be known ahead of his destination that he was to be expected, initially informing the ruler of Morocco of his plans as he plotted his route.

With the plans in place, the emperor, in all his ceremonial attire, rode his royally caparisoned steed on the most extravagant show across his lands and the Sahara Desert for Mecca, about 3,000 miles away. He was preceded by 500 heralds dressed in fine silks and brocade, each carrying a golden staff weighing 500 mithqals, and he was followed by 12,000 well-dressed slaves, each carrying four pounds of gold bars. There were baggage handlers and animal herders for the horses, oxen, cows and goats, and the bulk of the train consisted of 60,000 men, a suitable armed escort of soldiers, citizens with their retinues, and those managing the animals. Mansa Musa himself had 80 camels, each carrying 50-300 pounds of gold dust. There were many bands of musicians placed along the caravan to entertain and keep time.

The entire group left from Niani, heading west to Walata via Taghaza through Tuat. At Tuat, there was an unfortunate delay as the people tried to deal with an outbreak of "Pulex Penetrans," an infection of the feet that affected about half the caravan. By the time they proceeded to Wakala and then reached Ghadames, four months had gone by. Every Friday, Mansa Musa would make arrangements for a mosque to be built at any village he passed to mark his progress; including at Goundam and Doukoure. He would donate enough money for the material, the building supplies, and labor required to ensure it was completed.

There are some discrepancies in the available records of the journey. Most observers commented on his great generosity in handing out alms to the poor he encountered on the way, so one or two personal accounts of his relative meanness in this regard should be questioned as this is in conflict with the general picture. He was, after all, financially responsible for the general upkeep of the entire hajj, which must have cost a fortune in any case.

After a brief rest, they set off from Ghadames on the perilous trip across the Sahara, arriving in Cairo three months later to a tumultuous reception. The procession that entered the city presented a triumphant spectacle of wealth, color, pomp and circumstance displayed in the flags of the many districts represented, the musical accompanists of several orchestras, gymnastic displays, slave dancers arrayed in feathers and little else, and songs and recitations of their adventures by the many "griots" in the company. The pilgrims built a tented city in the vicinity of the Sphinx and settled in for a respite of three months.

Not much is known about Mansa Musa's personality, but it is apparent that he was very much concerned about the acknowledgement of his elevated status. Most people who had an audience with him were required to observe strict protocol, which included kissing the ground at his feet and throwing dust over their own heads. He did not speak to them directly, only through his interpreter, and he gave all his orders through his own staff. All this protocol was observed during his long and arduous hajj.

Mansa Musa was eagerly awaited in Cairo, which was the seat of the mighty Sultan Al-Nasir Muhammad. Emir Abu, the sultan's representative, went out to meet Mansa Musa and was received cordially. He wanted to present Mansa Musa formally to the sultan and invited him to an audience. Considering the fact that one of Mansa Musa's goals of the hajj was to impress his own authority on the rest of Africa and the world, it was surprising that he declined to go and meet the sultan. Emir Abu was not pleased, as protocol required Mali's emperor to accept the invitation. Mansa Musa gave as his excuse that he wanted nothing to deflect his interest from his pilgrimage.

Al-Umari, an Arab traveler and historian, described the encounter in Emir Abu's words:

> "[T]he audience was repugnant to him because he would be obliged to kiss the ground and the sultan's hand. I continue [sic] to cajole him and he continued to make excuses but the sultan's protocol demanded that I should bring him into the royal presence, so I kept on at him till he agreed.
>
> "When we came in the sultan's presence we said to him: 'Kiss the ground!' but he refused outright saying: 'How may this be?' Then an intelligent man who was with him whispered to him something we could not understand and he said: 'I make obeisance to God who created me!' then he prostrated himself and went forward to the sultan. The sultan half rose to greet him and sat him by his side. They conversed together for a long time, then sultan Mansa Musa went out. The sultan sent to him several complete suits of honour for himself, his courtiers, and all those who had come with him, and saddled and bridled horses for himself and his chief courtiers…"

Mansa Musa sent many loads of gold dust and unworked gold bars to the sultan's treasury and also showered all the senior court officials with generous gifts of gold and jewelry. When the hajj arrived in Cairo, the gold price was at a high of 25 dirhams per mithqal, and not surprisingly, the traders and stall owners in Cairo could not resist putting up the prices of all their goods in the face of the influx of 60,000 pilgrims shopping for gifts and curios. The expedition also replenished provisions by paying in gold, to the extent that by the time the hajj moved on, the price of one mithqal was well under 22 dirhams, resulting in an unstable gold market.

A meeting between Mansa Musa and the sultan ultimately took place in July 1324, probably on July 19, before they left Cairo and set off for Medina to pray at the tomb of the Prophet, the second holiest Islamic site. Mansa Musa offered 40 mule loads of gold dust at the Prophet's tomb.

The great hajj made a further 10 stops along the Red Sea to finally enter Mecca. In Mecca, all people are equal before God and their finery was discarded for the prescribed white, seamless garments symbolizing this and the prescribed rituals were observed. According to *The Chronicle of the Seeker*, "It is said that he asked the Shaykh of the noble and holy city of Mecca, may Almighty God protect it, to give him two, three, or four sharifs …[exhalted ones] of the kin of the Prophet of God, may God bless him and save him, to go with him to his country, so that the people of these parts might be blessed by the sight of them and by the blessing of their footsteps in these lands…"

The Shaykh was not prepared to give such an instruction, but he gave Mansa Musa permission to make the request himself. Mansa Musa instructed the town crier to offer any sharif who would be prepared to accompany him back to Mali 1,000 mithqals of gold each. Four freedmen of the tribe of Quraysh responded positively, so they, with their families, joined the pilgrimage and returned to Cairo to prepare for the trip home.

As this suggests, Mansa Musa recruited many gifted and professional people to return to Mali with him during the journey, including artists, writers, scholars and architects. Among these was the Andalusian poet, jurist and architect Abū Ishāq al-Sāhili. Mansa Musa also collected many of the latest books on a vast array of subjects, particularly philosophy, mathematics, the law, and medicine.

In fact, Mansa Musa had observed "zakat," the third Pillar of Islam which requires the giving of arms to a worthy cause, so well that by the time he reached Cairo, he had to borrow a huge sum of money from the money lenders to get himself and his monumental entourage home. By the time he returned to Cairo, the money market was severely depressed and the price of gold was extremely decreased. Realizing that this was mainly a result of his visit, he borrowed an enormous amount at inflated interest rates, which then caused gold to spike, and he subsequently repaid this loan all in one tranche when he reached home. This confounded all the money lenders in Cairo, and the influx promptly caused the gold price to crash again. The instability in the market was still evident 12 years after Mansa Musa's hajj, meaning he singlehandedly destabilized the Mediterranean's financial markets for over a decade.

For the route back from Mecca, Mansa Musa initially retraced his footsteps, but during the journey he received news that General Sagmandia had dealt with an uprising in Gao and had captured the city in 1325, thereby acquiring extensive and valuable territory. Mansa Musa diverted the hajj to Gao to assert his authority and received the king's two sons, Ali Kolon and Suleiman Nar, as hostages. They ultimately joined Mansa Musa's household and were brought up and educated as his own.

Mansa Musa also decided to annex Timbuktu, an important trading center located close to the bend in the Niger River, which put up little resistance. Many of the pilgrims were weary of travel, and some of the camels and horses were also exhausted. At Timbuktu's port of Kabara, most of the women boarded vessels to sail home to Niani on the Niger, and the rest of the party continued the journey by land. However, one of the vessels was attacked by the Lord of Dienne, a vassal state near the town of Kami, and the travelers, including the Quraysh families, were abducted. Luckily, the leaders discovered the prisoners' social status and released them in a place called Shinshin. Their descendants can still be found in this area in modern Mali.

Mansa Musa's hajj had succeeded beyond his wildest dreams, and he returned to a stable and extended empire, so he proceeded to execute an adventurous building programme in the country with some of the best architects in the world. He established universities and madrasas in Djenne and Segou. Stories of his great piety and wealth spread around the world, and Timbuktu was recognized as a trading destination by Venice, Genoa and Granada. Formal ambassadors from Mali were dispatched to Egypt, Arabia, and Morocco.

The first time Mali appeared on a European map was in 1339, and in 1367 a map showed a route from North Africa through the Atlas Mountains to the Sahara. In 1375, the great Jewish cartographer, Abraham Cresques, produced an Atlas of Africa that was commissioned by Charles V of France and took several years to execute, consisting of six parchment-covered wooden panels. The Kingdom of Mali is shown with a splendid black king seated on a raised throne, holding a gold tipped scepter and gazing at a large gold disc. Timbuktu (Tenbuch) is noted on the map.

As one source noted, "The Catalan Atlas stands in marked contrast to earlier medieval maps of Africa, which are filled with monsters, beasts, and grotesques — the farther from Europe, the more outlandish the representations of nature and humankind. Like medieval wonder books, those maps offered an Africa filled with men without noses and ants as big as dogs. By contrast, the Catalan Atlas sports delicate palm trees, tents of nomads, and surprisingly realistic elephants and camels." This beautiful atlas can still be seen in the Bibliothèque Nationale de France in Paris.

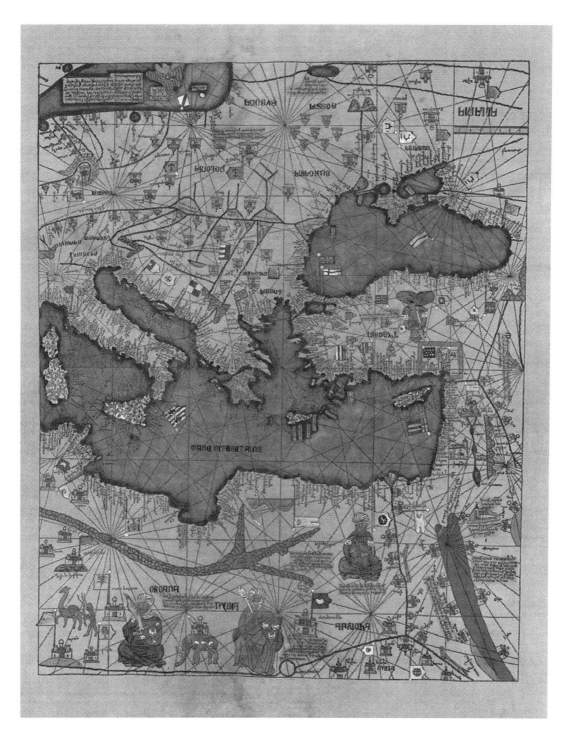

The Catalan Atlas

Timbuktu

"During his Moroccan exile, Ahmed Baba longed for his home country. He wrote, "O you who go to Gao, do so by way of Timbuktu and murmur my name to my friends. Give them the fragrant greetings of an exile who sighs after the soil where his friends, his family and his neighbors reside." - Ahmed Baba al-Massufi, a 16th century Berber scholar

Many people still believe Timbuktu is a myth, but it played a spectacular part in the history of West Africa. It was first settled by the wandering Berber and Tuareg tribes around 1106 as summer grazing for their large herds, and even then it was a crossroads for travelers. Once the summer was over and they moved the herds away, they left a slave woman named Tinbuktu there to look after their camp and watering well. That is one of the stories about how Timbuktu came by the name. Another source says that the caretaker's name was Buktu and that "tin" means a "water-well," which was one of the villages' major attractions.

Even in the early days, Timbuktu had two mosques and a thriving marketplace, especially for salt, which was very scarce in that part of Africa. Apart from offering services for the huge land caravans that rested there, there was also a river lifeline for every conceivable kind of good. The Niger River, one of the two great rivers in West Africa, has its headwaters in the Guinea highlands, and it follows an extended crescent, north east through Mali, Niger, Nigeria and the Niger Delta to discharge in the Gulf of Guinea. At the zenith of the crescent, the "Boucle du Niger," it turns sharply north and can spread 100 miles from its banks during flooding seasons. Near the bend is Port Bakara, with Timbuktu about three miles away. Even in Mansa Musa's time it could still be reached by pirogues during the Niger floods, and much of the wealth of Mali came from the alluvial panning of the headwaters of the Niger. The source of the Niger was only finally established in November 1830 by the explorers Richard and John Lander, who boated down the river from Bussa and got lost in the lush mangrove swamps as they struggled towards the sea.

Mansa Musa's Mali had 400 cities that connected all parts of his enormous empire, but he concentrated his efforts on making Timbuktu the centerpiece of his building programme. He commanded Abu Es Haq al-Sãhili to build him a great palace, the Madugu, and three new major mosques in the city.

The Djinguereber Mosque was one of al-Sãhili's real masterpieces and still stands today. The architect was given 12,000 mithqals of gold dust for his design of just this mosque, built in 1327 which could accommodate 2000 people and has three inner courts. It became the heart of the trading center that grew into the major commercial center in West Africa for decades. Despite, or maybe, because of the gifted architect, this great house of prayer was built of traditional and extremely cheap material: plain mud bricks. Mud or clay from a riverbed is mixed with some binding material, for instance, husks of rice or straw which is shaped into bricks and dried in the sun. This is called "adobe" or "banco." The walls are constructed with this material with wooden supporting beams running through the building from one outer wall to another. The structure is then "plastered" with a layer of mixed earth and water. The beams of wood often extend from the exterior walls and can be used for decoration or as scaffolding for later maintenance which is essential to keep the structure sound. Adobe is very heat proof and provides a pleasant interior and the conical minaret can be seen from any part of the city.

An early 20th century picture of the Djinguereber Mosque

Modern pictures of the Djinguereber Mosque

The Sankore Mosque was actually founded in 989 by the Chief Judge of Timbuktu, Al-Qadi Aqib ibn Mahmud ibn Umar. He built the inner courtyard to the same measurements as the Kaaba in Mecca, so by the time Mansa Musa was redeveloping the city, it was already the mainstay of the university. It is not certain to what extent it was refurbished or perhaps extended by al-Sãhili, but it certainly prospered and became an internationally acknowledged seat of academic excellence well into the 16th century.

An early 20th century postcard of the Sankore Mosque

Baz Lecocq's picture of the Sankore Mosque

The Sidi Yahya Mosque's year of construction is still debated because the dates given for its construction vary greatly. The date ranges from 1400-1450, which is much later than Djinguereber, but it is often mentioned along with Sankore as one of three mosques designed by al-Sāhili. Whatever the chronology, for many years Sidi Yahya formed part of the famous Mali University of Sankore. The large, covered prayer hall is oriented north to south and is supported by three colonnades. Two of the inner courtyards became cemeteries for local imams and other important religious figures so it was a venerated destination for pilgrims. It also had attractive decorated wooden doors.

These three mosques and the attached madrasas together became the great University of Sankore, which produced many exalted scholars and attracted world class teachers. At its height, the university had 25,000 students, and books became the most traded item in Timbuktu. Leo Africanus, a medieval traveler, wrote, "The rich king of Timbuktu has many plates and sceptres of gold... he keeps a magnificent and well furnished court... There are numerous doctors, judges, scholars, priests – and here are brought manuscript books from Barbary which are sold at greater profit than any other merchandise." Another source noted that Sankore had upwards of 70,000 works in its libraries.

At the university, major subjects were Islamic and Qur'anic studies, jurisprudence, and literature, and other important subjects included medicine, astronomy, mathematics, physics and chemistry, philosophy, linguistics and languages, art, history, and geography. Students were also required to follow at least one practical trade subject, such as tailoring, shoe making, or navigating. The lingua franca was Arabic and every student had to memories the Qur'an.

It could take 10 years of study before a student was invited to take the examination for a superior degree roughly equivalent to a Ph D. When they came to write the exam, the scholar was given a turban, which was wrapped in a special way to represent God with the turban point left hanging in the front. After they had finished the exam, the turban was pulled off and they had to undergo an oral examination. If the answers were satisfactory, the turban was returned and the student was considered to have passed.

One of the most famous students was Ahmad Baba al-Massufi, born in Timbuktu on October 26, 1556 into a family with a tradition of judges. By then, the University of Sankore was in full flower and he studied grammar, theology, and mysticism for 10 years before graduating cum laude. He quickly acquired a reputation for his mental acuity and was considered an outstanding intellectual. When the Moroccan Sultan Ahmad al-Mansur's forces conquered the city in 1591, Ahmad Baba was 30 and was very vocal in his opposition to the invasion. Within two years he was arrested and sent with his family to Marrakech. He was told he would be released if he agreed not to leave the city. This virtually made him a slave of the regime. He agreed reluctantly for the sake of his family and was soon teaching grammar, rhetoric and theology at the University of Marrakech. He produced a significant oeuvre during this, time writing 29 of the 56 titles attributed to him, before he was released and allowed to return home in March 1607. He continued to teach and write, and he became widely admired across Africa for his knowledge of the law. He also specialized in delivering meticulously argued fatwas. He was the Chancellor of Sankore University when he died in 1627, and he left many disciples in his wake, making him one of the great African intellectuals of the era.

In 1330, Timbuktu was attacked by Mossi, the Berber leader from the north, and Mansa Musa mobilized a force to take back this important city immediately. After taking it back, he fortified the walls to prevent any further attacks and spent the rest of his life improving the city, including expanding the university until it drew scholars from the entire world.

It is not known exactly when or how Mansa Musa died, but there is some consensus that he died in 1337, because his son Maghan was proclaimed ruler that year. Despite having kept the empire together while his father was on hajj, Maghan was an ineffective ruler and was succeeded by his uncle, Sulayman, in 1341. For his part, Sulayman was a mean-spirited man who did not command the respect of his brother.

In short order, Mali began to unravel and became threatened by the rise of the Songhai and Sunni Ali, a descendant of Ali Kolon, the young prince who had been taken as a hostage and educated in Niani when Mansa Musa had conquered Gao. Ali Kolon had escaped back to Gao in 1355 and established the Sunni dynasty, which would become the next base of power in West Africa.

Marauding Tuaregs regained control of Timbuktu by 1433, and by 1468 it was under the power of Sunni Ali the Great. The intellectual scholars and teachers immediately became suspect and were not well treated, but its international reputation did not suffer irreparably.

Upon Sunni Ali's death, one of his generals, Mohammed Ture, took power. Unlike Sunni Ali, he was a devout Muslim and in 1493 he established the Askia dynasty. He ruled with wisdom, and over the next 100 years Timbuktu reached its highest glory as one of the outstanding centers of academic scholarship in the world. A vibrant and skilled solid support base emerged in the town, and the trade of paper, ink, writing utensils, illustrators, binding services and the like were all available and provided profitable employment. The writing tool was the "calamus," made from a local shrub and about 12-16 centimeters long, or a bird quill. Ink was made from gum and charcoal, usually black or red with iron rust added to make it more permanent. All the ink in use at that time was acidic, which led to the inevitable deterioration of the paper. All the buildings comprising the University of Sankore were maintained or renovated by Imam Al Aqib, the Qadi of Timbuktu, from 1570-1583.

Unfortunately, savage attacks by the conquering Moors in 1591 were devastating. Libraries were looted, scholars were dragged off to exile in Morocco, and the families that managed to remain had to literally hide their entire book collections to keep them safe. Many also sent their precious manuscripts to family members who lived elsewhere, and those who fled either took their books with them or buried and secreted their personal manuscript collections in hiding places such as underground caves or disused wells. There was a decline in scholarship, and Timbuktu and the entire area suffered through tribal and religious upheaval and warfare until it was all but covered by sand.

In conjunction with that, there was a slow but steady decline in the Trans-Saharan trade that had long been the lifeblood of this part of Africa. The Tuaregs no longer protected the trade caravans or oases, instead turning to robbery and contributing to the increasing insecurity. Increasing colonization also played an important role, as Europeans focused on trading to the west across the Atlantic.

News from the "Dark Continent" appeared in a few odd reports from the last of the great explorers. One of them was Mungo Park, who was trying to chart the course of the River Niger for the British African Association. He made trips in 1795 and 1805, but he was unsuccessful in his quest and died in Nigeria. In 1824, the Société de Géographie offered 10,000 francs to the first non-Muslim to locate the "lost city of Timbuktu," and the Scottish explorer Gordon Lang lost his life in August 1826 attempting to do so. The prize was claimed by René Caillié, who entered Timbuktu disguised as a Muslim before returning to France in 1828. The Niger was still fairly navigable at this time, and Henry Barth, also traveling for the British African Association, actually lived in Timbuktu for a few months in 1853. He cultivated a friendship with one of the local scholars, Ahmed Al Bakkai, who afforded him protection. German Oskar Lenz and Spaniard Cristabal Benétez also returned with accounts of the exotic and legendary city in the late 1800s.

Park

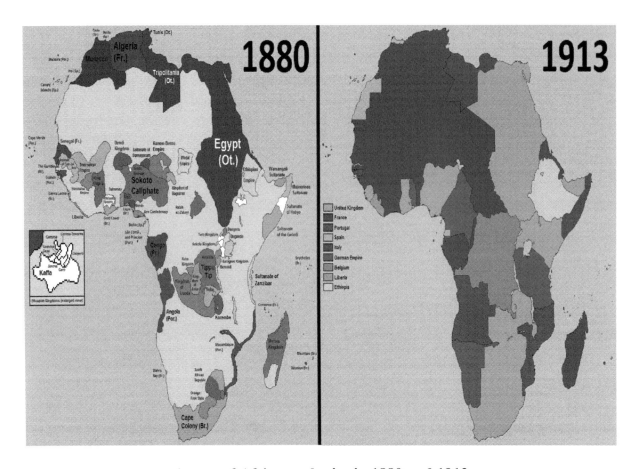

A map of African colonies in 1880 and 1913

On the morning of Saturday, November 15, 1884, plenipotentiaries of all of the major powers of Europe gathered at the official residence of the German Reich Chancellor, Prince Otto von Bismarck. As each entered the yard, they were met at their carriage door by the Chancellor himself and then ushered into the library, where an informal reception took place. Then, as a body, they climbed the wide, ceremonial staircase to a second-floor reception room, where each took his allocated seat at a semi-circular table arranged before a large and detailed map of Africa pinned to the wall. Bismarck addressed the assembled delegates, outlining briefly the objectives of the meeting, after which, casting his eyes from left to right, he declared the Berlin Conference formally in session.

Bismarck

A depiction of Bismarck at the Berlin Conference

The Berlin Conference of 1884-85, a dry and rather formal affair, was nonetheless one of the most important and far-reaching gatherings of international power to take place at any time during the 19th century, and one that would deeply impact the course of European and African history up to the present day. In its simplest terms, the Berlin Conference sought to regulate the subdivision of Africa between the principal European powers in a manner that would not cause a major war between them. Only a somewhat desultory European interest had been shown in Africa to date, amounting to little more than a patchwork of competing spheres of influence. These were mostly private concerns — chartered companies displaying a national flag — but here and there, territories were being annexed and occupied, and in general, a rather unhealthy mood of competition was incubating over the question of Africa.

Mali was annexed by French soldiers under Gaston Boiteaux on December 15, 1893, and it became part of French West Africa. In 1960, it became independent as the Republic of Mali. The leader, Modibo Keita, turned to the USSR for support, but the country did not thrive, particularly in terms of the Tuareg tribes who constantly felt underrepresented in the negotiations and the socialist structure. Many disillusioned Tuareg rebels were hired by and received training from Libya's Muammar Gaddafi. After his downfall, the fighters and their arms and equipment found a home among militant groups roaming the Sahel.

In 1968, Lieutenant Moussa Traoré took power in Mali by force. His problems were exacerbated by a tremendous drought in the 1970s, and a transition to democracy in 1992 brought Alpha Ounar Kounaré to power. By then, Mali was one of the poorest countries in the world, and the level of the River Niger had dropped so much that the remaining inhabitants in Timbuktu were dependent on UNICEF for food and water.

In 2002 Amadou Touré was elected president and attempted reconciliation by appointing a Tuareg as his Prime Minister. Unrest continued, but Touré was reelected by 71% of the electorate in 2007. Despite this, he was deposed in a coup in 2012, which resulted in Sharia law being imposed and many Christians fleeing the country. Gao, Kidal, and Timbuktu were taken by the rebels led by the National Movement for the Liberation of Azawad (MNLA) and the Ansar Dine party (Defenders of the Faith) led by Iyad Ag Ghali. Before long, the MNLA and Ansar Dine had turned on each other and several other radical Islamist groups, including Al-Qaeda, entered the fray.

While international bodies were debating what to do, the MNLA and Ansar Dine rampaged into Timbuktu in January 2013 and, armed with chisels, pickaxes and hoes, destroyed many shrines and severely damaged two major mosques, declaring them idolatrous under the Sufi interpretation of Islam. They returned to attack the recently built Ahmed Baba Institute, which had been specifically designed to protect the thousands of university and private manuscripts that had been collected together. At an opening of an exhibition of some of these manuscripts, Igo Diarra, Director of the Center d'art La Medina, said, "Our great poet Albakaye Ousmane Kounta of Timbuktu, loved to say that only knowledge could give true honour to tomorrow's youthful nation, bringing pride to their fathers and kin... That we should all attain such honour in life, so that together we may build one of the most beautiful bridges in the world: a bridge of ink and paper."

President Traoré, who had taken over just after the coup, requested help from France. The French launched Operation Sérval on January 11, 2013 and restored some kind of order, leaving 10,000 UN peacekeepers to keep civilians as safe as possible. The heritage sites that had been destroyed were rebuilt, and in 2016 the International Criminal Court, (ICC) sentenced Ahmad al-Mahdi to eight years in jail for leading the ransacking of the city of Timbuktu, an unprecedented finding.

Despite this dynamic and the progress achieved, the unstable security situation still remains an important concern, all the more so since the military presence and the vibrations caused by the military vehicles constitute a new threat to the buildings. It is recommended that the State Party, in consultation with the United Nations Multidimensional Integrated Stabilization Mission in Mali (MINUSMA), study reorganization options for traffic adjacent to the listed buildings in order to reduce the potential negative effects.

As all these events make clear, Mansa Musa left an enormaous legacy. He certainly did put medieval West Africa "on the map," in print and literally, as evidenced by the enormously lucrative Trans-Saharan trade routes that developed in the early part of his reign and expanded sharply after his pilgrimage to Mecca. By the time he died, the trade routes included destinations in East Africa, Saudi Arabia, the Mediterranean Sea, Morocco, and Europe. In the same vein, he also facilitated the extensive spread of Islam across the huge empire by being a devout Muslim who led by example and respected the right of every person to find their own way to God.

Most importantly, Mansa Musa's reign was marked by peace and stability, which allowed all his subjects to prosper. He demonstrated the power of wealth, the ability to move markets, the choice to reduce poverty, and the promotion of culture and scholarship. Not only did he send Malian students to distant universities to study, he also recruited teachers, architects, scholars, gifted craftsmen and professionals to return to Mali and make it their home. All of this helped establish Timbuktu as a center of learning and scholarship in Africa that drew students, teachers and visitors from around the world, and many of the manuscripts that made up the library of the University of Sankore survived. Since the mid-20th century, curious people have started to evaluate their contents, leading modern historians to reassess the development of the continent of Africa. Their very existence has turned the history of Africa on its head by indicating that Africa has a written record and an impressive scholastic heritage

UNESCO had a meeting in Timbuktu in the late 1960s to discuss a publication on the history of Africa, and one of the results of this meeting was that the Government of Mali established a center for the preservation of the remaining manuscripts. It was largely funded by Kuwait and a programme was developed at what was named the Ahmed Baba Center for Documentation and Research in 1973. Dr. Mahmoud Zouber, the center's first director, reviewed the library of the University of Sankore. He also recruited a retired teacher and local scholar, Abdul Kader Haidara, to help him locate the hundreds of privately held books and manuscripts that had been scattered and hidden in times of danger. Some collections had even been hidden during the French colonial era and had subsequently been lost.

When funding was available and the discovered work was significant, Abdul Haidara would purchase the texts. He was persistent enough to travel to Niger, Senegal, Guinea, Algeria, and the Ivory Coast, adding just over 16,000 manuscripts to the collection by 2002. Just as Latin had been the language of scholarship in Europe, the majority of the Timbuktu manuscripts were in Arabic, but there were also texts in Songhai, Tamasheq, Hausa, and Fulfulde, and the subjects covered scientific inquiry, literature, especially poetry, intellectual discourse, philosophy, and the history of Islam and the Qur'an.

Timbuktu was first labeled a World Heritage in Danger by UNESCO in 1988 because of sand encroachment on the buildings, and in 1990, it was identified as a World Heritage Site. On a presidential visit to Mali in 2001, Thabo Mbeki noted, "Yet, little could prepare one for the excitement of visiting the modest building of the Ahmed Baba Institute. There we were shown medieval manuscripts which are without any doubt among the most important cultural treasures of Africa, forming as it were, the most integral part of a rich and diverse cultural heritage of the town that includes its historic mosques and architecture and its cultural traditions...We were astounded by the artistic beauty of the illustration and illumination of some of these documents, surely among the most exquisite we had ever seen."

Online Resources

Other titles about Africa by Charles River Editors

Other titles about Mansa Musa on Amazon

Bibliography

Anderson, James M. 2013 *Daily life through trade: buying and selling in world history.* Greenwood Press, California.

Bell, Nawal Morcos (1972), "The age of Mansa Musa of Mali: Problems in succession and chronology", International Journal of African Historical Studies, 5: 221–234, JSTOR 217515.

Chirikure, S. 2013. *Metals in past societies: a global perspective on indigenous African Metallurgy.* Science+Business Media. N.P.

Corpus of Early Arabic Sources for West African History. 1981. Levtzion, N and Hopkins, J. F. P. Eds. Cambridge University Press, Cambridge.

De Villiers, Marq, and Sheila Hirtle. Timbuktu: Sahara's Fabled City of Gold. Walker and Company: New York. 2007.

Goodwin, A. J .H. (1957), "The Medieval Empire of Ghana", South African Archaeological Bulletin, 12: 108–112, JSTOR 3886971.

Hunwick, John O. (1999), Timbuktu and the Songhay Empire: Al-Sadi's Tarikh al-Sudan down to 1613 and other contemporary documents, Leiden: Brill, ISBN 90-04-11207-3.

Hunwick, John O. 2013. *Timbuktu and the Songhay Empire.* Brill, Leiden.

Jeffreys, M D W. 1952. *Pulex Penetrans; the Jigger's arrival and spread in Africa* South African Journal of Science, v. 48, Sept. Johannesburg, DHET.

Kurlansky, Mark. 2003. *Salt: a world history.* Penguin. N.P.

Levtzion, Nehemia (1963), "The thirteenth- and fourteenth-century kings of Mali", Journal of

African History, 4: 341–353, doi:10.1017/s002185370000428x, JSTOR 180027.

Levtzion, Nehemia (1973), Ancient Ghana and Mali, London: Methuen, ISBN 0-8419-0431-6.

Levtzion, Nehemia; John F. P. Hopkins, eds. (2000), Corpus of Early Arabic Sources for West Africa, New York, NY: Marcus Weiner Press, ISBN 1-55876-241-8.

Muslim Heritage Website. The Foundation for Science, Technology and Civilization. *The University of Sankore, Timbuktu* by Zulkifli Khair. Manchester. United Kingdom. Available at: http://muslimheritage.com/article/university-sankore-timbuktu [07.04.2019].

Roberto, W. M., Closs, M. B. and Ronconi. B. A. 2013 *The Situation in Mali.* UFRGS Model United Nations Journal, v. 1. Available at: https://www.ufrgs.br/ufrgsmun/2013/wp-content/uploads/2013/10/The-Situation-in-Mali.pdf [08.04.2019].

The Chronicle of the Seeker. N.D. by Mahmud Kati. Extract from *Islam from Prophet Muhammad to the Capture of Constantinople* by Bernard Lewis, 1987, OUP. Available at: http://college.cengage.com/history/primary_sources/world/chronicle_of_seeker.htm [01.04.2019].

The lost libraries of Timbuktu. Video. Available at: *https://www.youtube.com/watch?v=0OOizS357h0* [10.04.2010].

The South Africa-Mali Project. Timbuktu manuscripts: a South African Presidential Initiative. A Nepad Cultural Project. [2003] The Presidency. Pretoria. Available at: https://www.gov.za/sites/default/files/gcis_document/201409/potimbuktu0.pdf [11.04.2019].

Free Books by Charles River Editors

We have brand new titles available for free most days of the week. To see which of our titles are currently free, click on this link.

Discounted Books by Charles River Editors

We have titles at a discount price of just 99 cents everyday. To see which of our titles are currently 99 cents, click on this link.

Made in the USA
Columbia, SC
10 October 2020